Succeed as a Chief Virtual Officer

Succeed as a Chief Virtual Officer

Setting Up a Successful Virtual Assistant Business

Sue L Canfield

Copyright © 2014 by Sue L Canfield.

All rights reserved.

No part of this publication may be reproduced, stored in any retrieval system, or transmitted in any form or by any means without the prior permission of the author.

Requests for permission should be directed to Sue@ChiefVirtualOfficer.com.

Who knows; if you ask nicely, we might send you a free copy of the digital version of this book.

Succeed as a Chief Virtual Officer

Setting Up a Successful Virtual Assistant Business

By Sue L Canfield

ISBN-13:

978-1495267437

ISBN-10:

1495267431

Printed in the United States of America

This book is dedicated to my husband, Joel D Canfield, who inspires me in everything I do.

"[This is] a must have book for any person looking to start a professional service business virtually. Thanks for making this book, I really enjoyed it."

Kim Beckers
Kim Beckers Services

"It is well written and easy to read. I like the humor and anecdotes that are used throughout."

Professor L. Smedley
Sacramento City College

Table of Contents

Introduction 1
    Who Is Behind Chief Virtual Officer? 1
    Why a Chief Virtual Officer? 1
    Using This Book 1

Chapter 1 3
Are You Chief Virtual Officer Material? 3
    Skills Training and Certification 6

Chapter 2 7
Setting Up Your Business 7
    Your Business Plan 7
    Your Marketing Plan and Calendar 9
    What Should You Charge? 12
    Sue's Experience with Rates 13
    Cheap Versus Quality and Consistency 14
    Accounting 17
    Policies and Procedures 17
    Oops! How to Handle Those Mistakes 17
    Procedures - Setting Your Hours and Expectations 19
    Do Your Clients Know When You Are Available? 23
    Communicating With Your Client 24
    Pre-Contract Questionnaire 25

> Questions from Prospects 26
>
> Phone Consultation 27
>
> Contract 27
>
> Review: Setting Up Your Business Checklist 29

Chapter 3 31

Identifying your Ideal Client and Target Market......31

> Are You My Ideal Client? 31
>
> Identifying Your Target Market 33
>
> You Are Not My Ideal Client! 34
>
> Ideal Client 35
>
> May Not Yet Be an Ideal Client 35
>
> We're Not a Good Match 36
>
> Letting Go 36
>
> Review: Identifying your Ideal Client and Target Market 38

Chapter 4 39

Marketing Your Services 39

> Signs a Business Owner May Need to Hire a Virtual Assistant 40
>
> 35 Projects A Virtual Assistant Can Complete In an Hour 42
>
> Take Three Steps to Get Your First Client 44
>
> Never Pass Up an Opportunity 47
>
> Basic Marketing Strategies 48
>
> Website..49

6 Tips for Your Website 49

Free Report 50

Blogging for Business 51

Three Keys to Successful Blogging: Reading, Commenting, Writing 51

How Do I Promote My Blog? 53

Finding Time to Write 53

What Do I Write About? 54

Promoting Your Blog Promote Your Blog Via Email 56

Promote Your Blog Via Online Business Networking Sites 56

Getting Your Blog Started Checklist 57

Social Media 57

Newsletter 58

Email Management Systems 59

Article Writing 59

Marketing Your Services Checklist 60

Review: Marketing Your Services 60

Referrals and Testimonials 61

Sub-Contracting 62

Savvy Subcontracting - Gain and Retain Clients by Subcontracting 62

Collaborating with Other Chief Virtual Officers 63

The Next Step 64
Useful Online Tools 65
Online Tools Sue Recommends 66
Appendix 67
Sample Marketing Plan 68
Sample Marketing Calendar 70
Sample of Pre-Contract Questionnaire 71
Sample Services Contract 72
Sample Blogging Questionnaire 78
Sample Self Promotion Questionnaire 80
Final Note: 83
BONUS #1 84
11 Ways a Virtual Assistant Will Help You Get More Done 84
Save Money & Increase Efficiency Using Pay-As-You-Go Shared Employees 84
Get the best help at a fair price 85
What to Look for in a Virtual Office Professional 86
What Can't a VA Do? 87
How to Make the Best Use of Your Virtual Assistant 88
The List: 11 Ways a Virtual Assistant Can Help You Get More Done 90

    Increase Your Energy and Your Profits While
    Contributing More 93

Bonus #2 96

    Chapter Seven: Customer Service 96

Contact 100

About the Author..101

Introduction

Who Is Behind Chief Virtual Officer?
Chief Virtual Officer Coaching for Virtual Assistants was founded in 2009 by Sue L Canfield. Sue has been a virtual assistant since 2005.

Why a Chief Virtual Officer?
My philosophy revolves around the idea that you, the virtual assistant, are a business owner. However, I've found that often business owners, and even virtual assistants themselves, view a virtual assistant (VA) as little more than another employee. This can make it challenging to convey the true value a virtual assistant can provide a business owner. It also makes it challenging for the VA to present their business in the best professional setting.

That's why I decided to call the VAs we coach Chief Virtual Officers. After all, you are the chief officer of your business. This title more accurately reflects the VA's position as a business owner. Throughout the book I will use the term Chief Virtual Officer interchangeably with virtual assistant.

Using This Book
There are highly motivated Chief Virtual Officers just getting started who right now are not looking for one-on-one coaching or just cannot afford to invest in a coaching program. They would like to

Sue L Canfield

be able to work through the basics of the coaching program on their own and at their own pace.

This books allows that and helps you develop the mindset needed to run a successful virtual assistant business. Once you have completed the book, I am available to answer questions or provide ongoing coaching at an affordable rate. The book has been designed with large margins and plenty of space to write notes.

Chapter 1

Are You Chief Virtual Officer Material?

Do you have what it takes to be a Chief Virtual Officer? If you are exploring the possibility of becoming a Chief Virtual Officer, this is the very first question you need to answer. If you've already decided this is what you want to do, this section may help you more clearly define what you need to do in order to be successful.

So how do you know if this is the right career for you to pursue? There are a variety of factors to consider. Some of these will be addressed in more detail in later sections of the book. For now, let's discuss some of the basics.

Do you enjoy working independently? This is a very important factor since you will be working alone and without much direction for the most part. A Chief Virtual Officer needs to be able to work on your own. Do you work in a busy office right now? Will you feel lonely and miss the camaraderie when you start working independently from home? If you do not honestly think you can work without the support of others, you may want to think long and hard about whether this is really the career for you. Of course there are ways to combat the loneliness and we will consider that in a later section.

Do you enjoy taking the initiative? This is closely related to being able to work independently. Much of the work a Chief Virtual Officer does requires taking the initiative and not just waiting on the client to give you a task. A successful Chief Virtual Officer will look for ways to help grow a client's business and this requires initiative.

Do you have the necessary skills? It is important that you have marketable skills. This does not mean you need to know everything or have knowledge of every technological skill. Technology is ever-changing; so we can learn as we go. However, you do need basic skills in order to get started. They include knowing how to run a business, basic knowledge of computer programs, particularly word processing and spreadsheet programs such as Microsoft Word and Excel, and basic knowledge of the internet. There are some great skills training programs for specific skills in the industry. If you have no work experience, these programs can be very useful. However, if you have at least 2-5 years of administrative assistant experience, you can start a business without the need to be certified in any of these programs.

Do you have the necessary equipment? A Chief Virtual Officer works in the virtual world of the internet. So you'll need a reliable computer, internet access, basic software programs and a telephone, at a minimum.

Do you understand what it means to be a business owner? Since you are running a business, you need a basic understanding of what that means. You need a business plan, a way to track income and expenses, marketing materials, etc. This workbook and our coaching program are designed to help you get a good understanding of what it means to be a business owner.

Checklist

Use this checklist to help you determine if you have what it takes to be a Chief Virtual Officer. Use the space after each question to make note things you may need to work on before launching your business.

Are you Chief Virtual Officer Material?

- Do you enjoy working independently?
- Do you enjoy taking the initiative?
- Do you have the necessary skills?
- Do you have the necessary equipment?
- Do you understand what it means to be a business owner?

Skills Training and Certification

It's not strictly necessary to take specific skills training or to get certified in some sort of training for virtual professionals. Many Chief Virtual Officers have no specific training or certification. Their years of experience as an administrative assistant have been all they needed to be a successful Chief Virtual Officer.

If you have little or no experience as an administrative assistant, you may consider getting some skills training and/or certification. You can find lots of online skills training. Local community colleges also offer courses for virtual professionals.

Sierra College in Sacramento, California offers a Virtual Office Professional Certification course. I personally know some of the professors at Sierra College and several students who have taken the VOP classes and can put you in touch with one of the students if you have questions you'd like answered.

Chapter 2

Setting Up Your Business

Now that you've determined you are Chief Virtual Officer material and have the skills needed, you're ready to take on that first client, right? Not yet. First you need to set up your business. Though you may add additional services and skills as you go along, you really need some important things in place before you begin in order to avoid some pitfalls.

Your Business Plan

You may not think you need a business plan. You may not want to spend the time to create a detailed plan. Perhaps you feel you'll never look at it again. Or you may feel, like many, overwhelmed with the idea of creating a 40-page document.

A business plan is vital to help you clearly define what your business goals are and where you plan on taking your business. You should look at it periodically. In fact, you should review, and possibly even rewrite, your business plan every year. It does not need to be a 40-page document. It can be as short as one sheet of paper.

Sue's Personal Experience

When I first started working as a virtual professional, I was just helping a friend. I didn't expect it to grow into a business. So many of these things that I recommend are based on my experience. I didn't have much of this in place when I first started. As my business grew, I saw the importance of putting into practice what I'm now preaching. When I did, I saw my client list and revenue increase.

I especially learned the importance of clearly defining expectations. When I first started with only one client, I could be available 24/7 and turnaround time on a project was immediate. As my client base grew, that expectation was no longer realistic. I had to make some adjustments and my clients graciously adjusted along with me.

If I had thought ahead and put into place my clear and realistic expectations to begin with, it would have been much easier to deal with the growing pains my clients and I felt.

The most important sections of your business plan should include:

Mission statement - a brief description of what your company is all about

Vision statement - a brief description of your vision for your company

Goals - your goals for the year detailing specific revenue and client goals and time frames

Strategies - a brief description of the strategies you will implement to accomplish your goals

Actions - detailed, specific actions you can take on a daily basis to fulfill your strategies and goals

Your business plan should be kept handy and referred to at least monthly. In particular, note the actions you plan on taking. Check monthly that you are staying on track and accomplishing your goals.

Your Marketing Plan and Calendar

A marketing plan helps you identify specific strategies and actions to take to market to your target audience. Use the goals, strategies, and actions from your business plan that are specific to your marketing efforts.

Again, this does not need to be a complicated, lengthy document. A short one- or two-page document with some basic information is all that is needed.

Your marketing plan can be as simple as four basic sections:

1. Goal: A paragraph or two explaining the goal of your marketing efforts for the year. You want to include specific dollar amounts, number of clients, dates, etc.

2. Target Market: A paragraph explaining who your target market is and what you do for them.

3. Marketing Strategies: A paragraph noting the specific marketing strategies you will use

4. Budget: A final paragraph about your marketing budget and any marketing tools you have created.

The **Appendix** has a basic sample marketing plan.

Using the marketing plan as a basis, we now move on to the marketing calendar. The marketing calendar has five main components:

1. Column for each month of the year

2. Column for the specific marketing strategy you will focus on in a month

3. Column to detail the specifics of that particular strategy

4. Column to note if you accomplished your goals for the month or not (indicate a + if you did meet your goals; a - if you did not)

5. Column for notes to indicate what worked, what didn't and what you would do differently next time.

The **Appendix** has a sample of the marketing calendar.

The Marketing Plan and Calendar should be kept readily available for easy reference. You may even want to post these in your office where you can see them at a glance. Take some time at the beginning of each month to review your marketing plan and calendar and note the specific strategy you want to work on for that month.

By posting your marketing calendar near your desk, you can look at it daily to make sure you do something each and every day toward your marketing strategy for the month.

At the end of each month, review your activities. Give yourself a grade based on how much effort you put into the strategy and the results. Then make brief notes of what worked, what didn't and what you would do differently. This will help you at the end of the year to create next year's marketing plan. You will see which strategies really worked that you want to continue putting time and energy into. You may also find some strategies weren't for you and discard them completely. Others may need adjustment and you'll try them again.

What Should You Charge?

This is one of the most difficult things to determine for many new Chief Virtual Officers. If you are just starting in your business, you may feel that you cannot charge a higher rate because you don't yet have any experience. How can you determine the rate you should charge?

Though we will not give you an exact dollar amount you should charge, there are some factors to keep in mind. You are running a business now and there are expenses to consider. If you plan to make this your full-time business and be your main source of income, you need to charge enough to cover any expenses, taxes, licenses, equipment, software, insurance, and vacation.

The amount you charge can influence a prospect's decision to hire you. Obviously, if your rate is unnecessarily high, prospects will look elsewhere. But what if your rate is too low? You may find that prospects don't take you seriously. They may feel you are not a professional and don't value your own services.

In addition to determining your flat hourly rate, you may want to consider discounted rates and package rates. In fact, some Chief Virtual Officers have chosen to only use package or per project rates and discard an hourly rate altogether.

For example, a client may only want a one-time project. Perhaps you are asked to take 200 handwritten contact names and addresses and create a spreadsheet of all that information that the client can then use to upload to an email management system. Rather than charging an hourly rate, you may choose to provide the service for a flat project rate.

Should you choose to charge a flat hourly rate, you may wish to offer a discount for retainer packages. Standard retainer packages may be for 5, 10, or 20 hours or more per month. A discount of 10%, 20%, and 25% may be given to clients who prepay retainer rates.

Sue's Experience with Rates

One of my first clients told me that if I had told him I only charged $15 an hour, he would have found someone else. He expected to pay at least $25 per hour and thought I should charge even more than that. He said that if I didn't think my services were worth $25 an hour, why should he value my services?

Another thing to consider is the fact that many prospects may not want to commit to a large chunk of time until they have had a chance to work with you and can see that you are a good fit. Consider offering a two-hour starter package.

Do some research in the industry and see what other virtual assistants, particularly in your area, are charging. That may give you a good indication of what prospects and clients are willing to pay. Do keep in mind though that the rate you decide to charge should reflect your value and not be determined solely by what other virtual assistants are charging.

Your rate needs to cover the costs of:

- Medical and other insurance costs
- Paid holidays, vacation, sick time
- Supplies
- Advertising costs, including website, brochures, postcards, postage
- Equipment and repair costs
- Self-employment, state and federal taxes
- Cost of living increases

Cheap Versus Quality and Consistency

You've set your rates as a virtual assistant and then are contacted by a prospect who wonders if you'll work for $4-$10 per hour. You know there is no way you can cover your costs for such a low hourly rate. How can you explain to a prospect why your rate is so much more and why they still may want to use your services?

I've talked with quite a few clients and prospects who have tried the $4-$10 per hour services and then decided to use a professional virtual assistant instead. The two main reasons: quality and consistency.

The cheaper service providers don't usually offer the same quality of service that a professional virtual assistant can provide. Small business people are looking for someone who not only can do the tasks assigned, but that can also add value. A professional virtual assistant can do this by doing additional research and making recommendations.

One client said, *"My only previous experience is with assistants that just did what I told them to, but contributed very little input and really didn't add any value."*

That client needed an email marketing tool and had just signed up with one of the email management services. Before we got started on the project I spoke with the client and asked enough questions to find out that the particular service he had signed up for was not going to meet his needs. I offered to do some research and make recommendations on what would work best for his needs.

After we found the right service for his business, this same client said, "I just love having an assistant that is knowledgeable and gives thoughtful consideration to our projects."

The other complaint business people had about the cheaper services was consistency. They didn't feel they always were working with the same person or getting the same level of service from each person. The availability of the service was inconsistent.

There may be times when using the cheaper services is right. Each person will need to make their own determination on that. I thought of something in my life to use as an example. Have you ever been to one of those stores where everything is only $1? I have too. In fact, there are many times when buying something there really cheap is just what I need. For example, I homeschool my daughter. At these stores I can buy all kinds of workbooks, stickers, pencils, glue, etc. for my five-year old to use in school projects. These projects aren't going to be saved in the Smithsonian. It also doesn't really matter if one week I go there and buy a pack of construction paper but the next week they don't have any. It seems that these stores are cheap but they don't necessarily have a consistent stock of items.

But let's say I need a quality gift. I could spend $5 at the cheap store and pick up several little gifts that might be fun to give to my five-year old. But would I buy a quality gift there to give to my friend as a going away present? No! I would go to a store where I could find something of quality, though I would expect to pay more, of course.

Then there's the inconsistency at these cheaper stores. I may be able to find the construction paper I want for a school project one week and then it's not there the next week. So if I really needed construction paper on a weekly basis, I'd be less inclined to go to the cheaper store because I wouldn't be sure I could always find it. I'd be more inclined to go to the local office supply store where they always have the paper I need.

So perhaps there is a time where using a cheaper service is the right choice. For the most part, though, business persons have found that paying a higher rate for a professional virtual assistant is the right choice because they get the quality and consistency they need.

Accounting

You may choose to have someone who specializes in accounting services actually handle your books. Or you may choose to do it all yourself to save money, particularly when you are first getting started. If you choose to do your own accounting and have no accounting experience, do some research and talk with someone in the accounting industry to determine what's best for you and your business.

An easy and affordable way to get started setting up your accounting is to use Quick Books Online. (http://quickbooksonline.intuit.com/) They have a free version just for invoicing and the basic package is only $9.95 per month.

Another easy way to bill your clients and get paid is to use PayPal.

Policies and Procedures

Customer Service Policy What happens when something goes wrong and a client is unhappy? Having a customer service policy in place can help prevent misunderstandings. When something does go wrong, your customer service policy makes clear to your client what you are going to do to make things right. Your policy should be a clear reflection of your values and ethics.

Oops! How to Handle Those Mistakes

It's bound to happen. We're only human and we all make mistakes. We try very hard in our businesses to put processes in place so that we don't make mistakes. But it happens. So what do you do when it happens?

Here's my opportunity to be authentic and admit that recently we made a mistake on a client project. Of course it was completely unintentional and accidental. Upon review we still don't even know how it could have happened. But it did. Our client brought it to our attention in a very kind manner. He knew it was accidental and unintentional. Though the mistake couldn't actually be fixed, he expected us to offer some sort of compensation for the error. And we completely agreed.

We were mortified that a mistake had been made! This client is one of our favorite clients. We really enjoy working with him and we weren't sure if this was going to be the end of our working relationship. We needed now to make sure we lived up to our customer service superheroes policy. So we discussed exactly what we could offer this client to make amends for this mistake. We wanted to be sure that what we offered far exceeded any expectations he had.

We called our client and apologized for the mistake. No excuses. Then we explained what we could do to make amends. We made a generous offer of additional time at no charge and offered to take on a project we knew he needed done—at no charge. We wanted to make sure our client felt well taken care of and hoped he'd continue working with us.

Our client was very happy with our offer of additional work at no charge! He explained that he'd wondered how we would handle the situation. He realizes that mistakes happen and that it's the way they are handled that makes all the difference. He was very excited to continue working with us and had a project we could start on immediately. He was so impressed with the results of that project that he offered to write a testimonial if he hadn't already (he already had though). We continue to work together and our client continues to refer others to us.

Yes, we will make mistakes. It's how we handle them that determines the outcome. So here are my 3 simple rules on how to handle mistakes: 1. Own up to your mistakes. Take responsibility for what you did. Don't make excuses. Figure out how the mistake was made, if at all possible, and then put into place processes to prevent that mistake from happening again. 2. Apologize. Give your client a sincere apology, without excuses, for what happened. If you used a sub-contractor and the error was made by your sub-contractor, you still need to take responsibility. 3. Make generous amends. This does not have to be monetary. It can be additional time or product. Be sure your client feels they got more than enough compensation. If the error resulted in a $500 loss for your client, make amends of double that value. When you own up to your mistakes, apologize, and make generous amends, you'll find that your clients appreciate your openness, honesty and integrity.

Procedures - Setting Your Hours and Expectations Prospects want to know what to expect when they begin working with you. Many of these procedures can be posted on your website and should be included in your contract.

Procedures to include in your contract may be:

Days and hours you work. If you've chosen to work a four-day work week and take Mondays off, make that clear before the client signs the contract. If they are not aware of that fact and send you a task to do on Friday that needs to be returned to them on Monday, they will be very disappointed and upset when you are not able to do it. Or you will be frustrated because you decide to go ahead and do the task to keep them happy though you would normally use Mondays to help out at your child's school.

Telephone and email availability. When will you be available to talk by phone or respond to voice mail and emails? You may choose to only be available by phone from 1-2 pm each work day. If so, make sure that information is clearly conveyed before the contract is signed. What is your policy regarding emails? Will you respond immediately or within 24 hours?

Turnaround time. When a client gives you a task, how long will it take to get done - 24 hours, a week, 10 days?

Confidentiality Clause. Most clients want to know that any information you have about their business remains confidential. Include a confidentiality clause in your procedures.

Work Flow. This may be customized for each client. Ask questions to find out what they expect. It may be that they would like a weekly phone call or a weekly report emailed to them detailing what you did and the time spent on their project. Perhaps they have a monthly task they would like you to remind them of. Note these details in the procedures section of your contract.

Procedures Checklist

(Fill in the information you want included in your contract)

Days and Hours Available

Monday   Hours

Tuesday   Hours

Wednesday   Hours

Thursday   Hours

Friday   Hours

Saturday   Hours

Sunday   Hours

Sue L Canfield

Telephone and Email Availability

Monday   Hours

Tuesday   Hours

Wednesday   Hours

Thursday   Hours

Friday   Hours

Saturday   Hours

Sunday   Hours

Turn Around Time

Task   (Ex.) Post a blog entry

Turnaround Time (Ex.) 24 hours

Confidentiality Clause

Work Flow

(Ex.) Email weekly report; Due each Friday by 5 pm

Do Your Clients Know When You Are Available?

Often, especially when a virtual assistant first starts their business, they may feel the need to work at all hours, even late into the night and on weekends. Of course that's the beauty of working for yourself; you can work those hours if you choose and take the more traditional hours to spend with your family.

However, do you want your clients thinking they can call you at 2 pm on a Saturday or email you at midnight and get a response at 6 am? Though you want your clients to feel that you are available, you need to set some guidelines as to when you are available and make sure all your clients are aware of this.

So I suggest you determine set hours that you are available for phone calls and make it clear when you will return emails. By clearly setting specific hours that you work on client projects, your clients will know when you are available and appreciate that. And you won't feel pressured to be up until midnight finishing a project since your clients know your work day ends at 5 pm.

One note of caution: as Chief Virtual Officers we may have clients in more than one time zone. Make it clear what hours you work in your time zone and be sure clients in different time zones are aware of the time difference.

Yes, let your clients know your available hours. Post your hours on your website and include it in your contract. Both you and your clients will appreciate it.

Communicating With Your Client

Be sure to communicate clearly with your client so everyone's expectations are met. Here are some things to discuss with your client.

- What hours are you available to work on client projects?
- What hours are you available for phone calls?
- When will you reply to emails?
- When is the best time to reach your client and for them to reach you?
- How does your client prefer to communicate? (email, telephone, instant messenger)
- Will you have daily, weekly, monthly updates by phone and/or email?

Pre-Contract Questionnaire

This questionnaire is designed for prospects to fill out before your first telephone consultation. Not every prospect will fill this out before contacting you. It can also be used as a tool to aid you in determining if this is the right client for you and in creating the contract.

The pre-contract questionnaire should include these sections:

- Prospect's name
- Company name
- Contact information including address, phone, cell phone, fax, email, website
- Industry
- Brief description of their business, including the years in business
- Brief description of the services they are looking for
- Questions prospect has about your services
- Days and times available for telephone consultation
- How the prospect heard about your services
- Name of person, if any, who referred the prospect

Questions from Prospects

Be prepared to answer questions a prospect may ask you. Use this page to write down your answers so you are quickly able to answer these questions when talking with a prospect.

- What do you do?
- Do you specialize in a particular task?
- Can you provide me with testimonials of other clients you've worked with in my industry?
- What services do you offer?
- What are your rates?
- Why should I choose to work with you?
- Why would I work you when I can find someone else at a much lower rate?
- Can you help me grow my business, and how?
- How do we get started?

Phone Consultation

Most prospects will want to speak with you by telephone. This enables you and your prospect to get to know one another and find out if you are a good match. Offer a free 30-minute phone consultation. That is usually more than enough time to answer all their questions and to find out if you are ready to take the next step of sending a contract.

During the phone consultation, you want to get more information:

- "Tell me more about your business and what you do."
- "Would you mind sharing some information about you personally - do you have children? What are your favorite hobbies?"
- "What are your business goals for the next six months?"
- "What are the first three priorities you'd like me to assist you with if we start working together?"
- "Tell me what your expectations are if we work together."
- "How many hours do you expect you will require each week or each month?"

Contract

A contract is vital in most business transactions. Before you begin work for a client, you need to have a signed contract in place. This prevents misunderstandings since everything is down in writing.

The basic components of a contract include:

- **All your contact information:** company name, your name, address, email, phone, fax, cell phone, website
- **Scope of work:** detailing exactly what type of services you are providing.
- **Financial obligations:** detailing rates and how and when payments will be made.
- **Work Flow:** detailing how the work will get done and turnaround times.
- **Policies and Procedures:** detailing your availability; include your customer service policy.
- **Confidentiality:** the very important confidentiality clause.
- **Termination:** detailing what happens should you or the client choose to terminate the contract.
- **Independent Contractor:** include language clearly stating that you are working as an independent contract and not as an employee. This will help avoid any confusion when it comes to tax time for both you and your client.
- **Signature and Date:** both you and the client should sign and date the contract. Electronic signatures are legally acceptable and binding.

A sample contract is included in the **Appendix**.

Now that you have your business plan, marketing plan and calendar, set your rates, set up a simple accounting process, written up your policies and procedures, and have a pre-contract questionnaire and contract ready, you are ready to consider if you need to hire outside help.

You may want to consult an attorney to make sure you have all your legal bases covered. Do you have a tax accountant that can help make sure your ducks are in a row when it comes time to file your taxes?

Have you considered hiring a business coach? Every great business coach I know has had a business coach. And successful Chief Virtual Officers often have a mentor or business coach.

Review: Setting Up Your Business Checklist

Are you ready to get started? Have you created your business plan, marketing calendar, determined your rates, created your policies and procedures, prepared for the phone consultation and created your contract?

- Business Plan
- Marketing Plan and Calendar
- Determining Rates
- Creating Policies and Procedures
- Preparing for a Phone Consultation
- Contract

Sue L Canfield

Chapter 3

Identifying your Ideal Client and Target Market

You may be thinking your client can be anybody. This is one of the biggest mistakes you can make. It's important to narrow your focus so you attract the clients you really want to work with. Prospects will know you are the Chief Virtual Officer for them when you clearly communicate who your ideal client is and your target market.

Are You My Ideal Client?
- Describe the type of person you enjoy working with? (Ex. upbeat, positive, looking for someone to partner with to help grow their business)
- Men, women? (Ex. women)
- What age group? (Ex. 40-50 years old)
- Is there a particular industry? (Ex. life coaches)

Compile your answers into a detailed, very specific description of your ideal client.

(Ex. My ideal client is a woman, 40-50 years old, who is upbeat, positive and looking for someone to partner with to help grow her life coaching business.)

Use this space to write your detailed description of your ideal client.

Identifying Your Target Market

Now that you've described your ideal client, you have a good idea of your target market. You may already have experience in a particular industry and choose to niche in that industry. For example, if you have experience in Real Estate, you may niche as a Real Estate Virtual Assistant.

Another way to determine your target market is to identify the types of tasks you enjoy doing or would like to learn more about. If you love creating ezines for health and fitness providers, you can target the health and fitness industry and niche in the particular task of ezines.

If there's a skill you'd like to learn and niche in, learn the skill. However, don't make the mistake of thinking you have to be an expert at every skill in order to be a Chief Virtual Officer. If you have only one special skill, you can niche in that and still be successful.

- What experience do I have? (Ex. real estate)
- What types of tasks do I enjoy? (Ex. creating ezines)
- What skill(s) would I like to learn? (Ex. autoresponders)

You Are Not My Ideal Client!

Perhaps you've spoken with a prospect by telephone and have agreed to send a proposal for their review. But your intuition is telling you that something doesn't feel right. Perhaps this is not your ideal client after all. Should you go ahead and sign this prospect on as a client just because you think you need the money? No!

One of the most important factors in working with someone is personality. For whatever reason, perhaps you and this prospect just didn't hit it off. If your intuition makes you feel that this just isn't a good match, listen to your intuition! Otherwise, you will regret it. Every single time my intuition made me feel like a particular prospect just wasn't right and I went ahead and decided to work with them, it was a mistake. So listen to your intuition. It's much easier to tell a prospect that you are not a good fit for each other than to tell a client that you are no longer going to work with them.

So before you decide to take on that client, ask yourself:

- Do you feel excited about the possibility of working with them?
- Do you feel comfortable with the tasks they want you to do and their expectations?
- Does this prospect's personality fit with yours?
- Do you feel you could work with this client on a long-term basis?

- Do you feel you can communicate freely with this client?
- Does the client understand your availability, policies and procedures?
- Can this client afford your services?
- Does your skill set match the client's needs?

Ideal Client

- Client is able to clearly communicate their business goals.
- Client is looking for a long term relationship.
- Client communicates regularly with the VA.
- Client understands virtual assistants often work with several clients and has realistic expectations.
- Virtual Assistant is excited about the type of work Client does.
- Virtual Assistant is excited about the prospect of working with the Client.

May Not Yet Be an Ideal Client

- Client is vague about their business goals.
- Client questions the amount of time required to complete tasks.
- Client is too busy to return VA's phone calls and/or emails.
- Client sets unrealistic deadlines and expectations.
- Virtual Assistant does not enjoy Client's industry or the type of work Client does.

- Virtual Assistant's intuition is saying "we're not a good match".

We're Not a Good Match

No, you don't have to take on every prospect. You can say "no, we're not a good match." Recently a prospect asked me about my email management services. When I asked a few questions, I learned he wanted to email tens of thousands of people several times a week. He could not explain clearly how he acquired these contacts and did not want to pay for an email management system. It quickly became obvious that this prospect wanted a cheap way to spam people and hoped I would be able to help him. Besides not complying with the CAN-SPAM Act, this task went against my values and ethics. I explained to the prospect that there were certain laws that needed to be complied with and referred him to the CAN-SPAM Act. I also recommended that he look into an affordable email management system and explained best practices for acquiring valid contacts. Then I told him I wouldn't be able to help him. Simple as that.

Letting Go

Perhaps you signed on a client even though you had that feeling that this wasn't really a good match. You know that you are not enjoying the work anymore or working with this client. When that happens you don't do your best work. In fact, it affects the work you do for other clients as well. So it's time to let this client go. How do you do that?

There may be no specific reason you can identify for not wanting to continue to work with this client. Or there may be a very good reason. Perhaps they are constantly changing their mind. Perhaps they complain about the amount of time it took or how much the project cost, even though you detailed it in the contract. Perhaps they wait till the last minute and then just have to have something done even though they know it's after hours. Perhaps you started out doing certain tasks and now they want others and you just aren't comfortable doing those tasks.

Perhaps there's a different virtual assistant that would be a good match for them. Another VA may have the right personality, the right skill set, the right rates. If at all possible, help the client find the right VA for them when you let them know that you are not going to continue working with them.

When firing a client, remember to extend the same courtesy you would expect. Simply explain that this arrangement is not a match for you. If they press for details, be honest, and be polite. Chances are, they already know what's wrong.

Be sure to fulfill any obligations you made to the client before terminating your contract.

Review: Identifying your Ideal Client and Target Market
- Are You My Ideal Client?
- Identifying Your Target Market
- You Are Not My Ideal Client!

Chapter 4

Marketing Your Services

Your business is set up, you've identified your ideal client and target market and you're all set to open shop! How do you get your first client? You know you've got to market your services; but how? This is one of the most important aspects of business and the one area everyone asks about. There's a ton of information on marketing and with ever-changing technology, marketing continues to evolve. We will discuss some basic marketing strategies and encourage you to continually research and refine your marketing strategies.

Sometimes business owners aren't aware they need help. A successful Chief Virtual Officer educates business owners with information about how their services can benefit the business owner. One of the first steps is helping the business owner realize their need. You may need to find out if the business is showing signs of their need for help and point this out to the business owner.

Sue L Canfield

Signs a Business Owner May Need to Hire a Virtual Assistant

- Working long hours each day and still feeling behind.
- Unable to work on the business because they are too busy working in the business.
- Doing tasks that they do not like or are not very good at.
- Family members feel the business owner doesn't spend enough time with them.
- No time to pursue ideas for growing the business.
- Penalties and fees have been assessed because of falling behind in paperwork.
- The feelings of stress running a business outweigh the feelings of joy of owning a business.
- Technology that could streamline the business gets ignored because it seems overwhelming.

There are two questions we use to help prospects determine how best they can use our services:

1. What are the things you do that don't increase your energy? We all do things we really enjoy and that energize us. We also do things that tend to drain our energy. Those are the things we want to know about so we can help business owner with them.
2. What are the things you do that don't directly increase your profits? You know - those tasks that have to be done in a

business but don't directly bring in income. Again, those are things we can help them with.

Ask a friend in business if you can interview them and ask them these questions. Use the space below to note your answers.

Sometimes a prospect just needs some ideas of things you can do. Below is a list of projects a virtual assistant can accomplish, each usually within an hour. Providing your prospects with a similar list of tasks you can accomplish, each within an hour, will educate them in how best to utilize your services.

35 Projects A Virtual Assistant Can Complete In an Hour

1. Phone a minimum of 12 clients for a specific project.
2. Mail merge 50 letters including stuffing and mailing.
3. Create a viable prospect list of 25-30 contacts.
4. Create an Email campaign.
5. Data Entry of a minimum of 75 contacts in an Excel spreadsheet.
6. Create correspondence for a client or prospect.
7. Edit and proof a minimum of a five page report.
8. Setup the process for an ezine or newsletter.
9. Balance a monthly bank statement.
10. Update web site content.
11. Transcribe a half hour of audio.
12. Research for a specific project.
13. Type handwritten notes from a seminar.
14. Make edits to 1-5 web pages (depending on # of changes).
15. Post 3-4 blog entries.
16. Submit a press release to 5 sites.
17. Submit an article to 5 sites.
18. Do follow-up research on a client, prospect, applicant, or competitor.
19. Convert document files to PDF format.
20. Build a custom spreadsheet.
21. Proofread a narrative of up to five pages.
22. Edit and proof copy for five Web pages.

23. Make calls to confirm your appointments, engagements, or reservations.
24. Copy edit and proofread a brochure.
25. Stuff, seal, label, and stamp a bulk mailing of 50 letters.
26. Write a blog entry.
27. Analyze and update basic SEO elements for a 5 page website.
28. Create PDF's for numerous company documents, whitepapers, charts .
29. Set up a blogging account/program and add the link to the site menu.
30. Research best price/features for a needed service, technology, or item.
31. Maintain a Pinterest account.
32. Create and manage social media messages.
33. Create photo memes for use on Pinterest, blogs, and social media networks.
34. Create pull quotes from client's blog, website, book to use as marketing messages.
35. Use Client's contact list to invite contacts to connect on their social media networks.

This is a sampling of what a virtual assistant can do and serves as a guideline only.

Take Three Steps to Get Your First Client

The #1 challenge new virtual assistants have is getting that first client. You know that if you could get just one client and wow them with your work that they will in turn recommend you to their friends. But how do you get that first client?

There are a variety of things you could do. Here are three different steps you can take to find that first client.

Step #1: Subcontract for an established virtual assistant. Find an established virtual assistant and build a relationship. Some virtual assistants need additional help from time to time and if you've established a relationship, they may call on when they need extra help. Be aware, though, that the rate as a subcontractor may be significantly less than the rate you would charge a client directly. This is to be expected since as a subcontractor you did not go out and find the client and are not directly managing the project.

Subcontracting is a good way to gain experience and make a little income. I strongly suggest you have some sort of written agreement or contract clearly defining expectations and rate of pay. I know virtual assistants who only do subcontract work and don't want the additional responsibilities that come with managing the client directly.

Step #2: Trade or barter services. Especially in difficult economic times, many solo professionals are willing to trade or barter services. I've known life coaches, business coaches, massage therapists, chiropractors and other service providers that were willing to provide their services in exchange for a virtual assistant's time.

If you could use one of these services, find out if they would be willing to barter. Again, this is a great way to get experience and may result in good word of mouth referrals. If the client is happy with your work, this is a great opportunity to ask for a testimonial to use in your marketing materials.

Step #3: Offer an hour or two at no charge. Some prospects don't want to hire a VA unless they know the VA has hands-on experience and this is a wonderful way to get started. I know you're wondering right now if I really just told you to give away some of your time without getting paid. Is that what I meant? Yes! However, I did not say you wouldn't get anything in return. Let me explain.

You are brand new, just set up in business and have no clients, no testimonials, no proof you are good at what you do. So why would anyone want to hire you or retain your services for five or ten hours each month? But if you could get even one client, a glowing testimonial and begin your portfolio, then there's a reason for someone to consider using your services. So how do you get that first client? Offer an hour or two for free.

Of course you still want to have a contract detailing the work you will do in that one or two hours. Be sure that both you and the client have the same clear expectations. Let the client know up front that you'd like them to provide a testimonial - if they are truly pleased with your work.

If you provide excellent service, you will find that the majority of clients who you gave an hour or two of time at no charge will want to continue using your services and will gladly pay your fee. I have never been disappointed with my return on investment when I've done this. I've found it's very rare that a client uses their free hour or two and then never comes back.

Since many small business owners are still reluctant to use a virtual assistant and aren't sure what we can do for them, offering a small amount of our time can break the ice. In my opinion, this is not much different than a business coach who offers a free report with the hope that you'll then pay for the more extensive eBook or even pay for his business coaching.

If you're reluctant to offer free services to someone you don't know, you may find a friend or family member that you can do some work for to gain some experience. Of course, this can have challenges of its own.

So what step will you take to get your first client?

When you are looking for your first client, let everyone you know that you've started your business. Tell all your family, friends, the bank teller, people in the networking group, you dentist, neighbor, everyone. You may be surprised at who ends up contacting you because they heard from their dentist (who is also your dentist) that you provide ezine services and they've been looking for someone to help them with that.

Never Pass Up an Opportunity

Here's an interesting story of how one of my clients hired me to help with her marketing efforts. One day I found a flier on my front porch. I was impressed with how the flier looked and the information found in it. It was put out by a local real estate agent and her email address was on the flier. I emailed her and let her know how impressed I was with the look of the flier and with the information in it. We ended up corresponding by email and once she found out what services I offered, she let me know that she needed some help putting out the next flier. We ended up working together and I've really enjoyed working with her.

Basic Marketing Strategies
- Website
- Free Report
- Blog
- Social Media
- Newsletter
- Article Writing

List below other marketing strategies you want to explore using.

Website

Every business owner should have a website. Your website can provide lots of valuable information for prospects. All your printed marketing materials should have your web address. Any online profiles you have should also include your web address.

6 Tips for Your Website

1. Get professional help to build or update your website. If you already know how to create a professional-looking website, that's great! But if you don't and are trying to build a site for the first time with tools you are not familiar with, you're likely to end up with an amateurish-looking website. Do your research and get references from the web designer.
2. Write your web copy to reflect who you are. Write about yourself using 'I' and 'my'. You are a service provider and as such need to sell yourself. You need to develop a trusting relationship with your prospective client. This can only happen if they can learn more about you, who you are, what you like. Write about yourself, why you chose to be a VA, a bit about what you enjoy doing. This helps your prospect get to know you, feel comfortable and come to trust you.
3. Use your photo. There will be a stronger connection and feeling of trust if a client

can at least see your photo since you may never meet in person.
4. Be consistent. You need a consistent look on your website, on each page, and in your navigation. Otherwise your visitor may get confused or at least feel disconnected as they navigate through your website. This includes using the same color theme and basic layout on each page.
5. Provide valuable content. Don't just copy every other VA's site with "What's a VA?" or "List of Services". Create information that's specific to your target so they'll be educated and know that you're the right person for them.
6. Post your rates. Some VAs don't post specific rates and only refer to vague discounts. Don't surprise your prospects with your rates when they contact you. Let them know up front what to expect. Make sure to calculate an appropriate rate. You may want to speak to a business coach or another experienced VA to find out how to determine an appropriate rate.

Free Report

Marketing should be educational. To convert a prospect to a client, you need to let the prospect learn about you, come to know the type of person you are, so they can come to trust you and want to work with you. One of the best ways to educate prospects is to offer a free report. Post it at your website. You may offer it as a bonus for signing up for your newsletter. This allows you to stay in touch with prospects so they can learn even more about the benefits you can provide.

Blogging for Business

Blogging is one piece of the puzzle in your marketing strategy. You may feel overwhelmed with the idea of blogging and are unsure where to begin. Since blogging is marketing, it is important to think of blogging as a tool to educate your prospects and clients. Your willingness to share valuable information on your blog with your prospects before you ever ask them to use your services builds a relationship. As with all marketing strategies, consistency is important. That means you must be consistent in your blogging also. Once you get started, set up a strategy to continue posting blog entries on a regular basis.

Three Keys to Successful Blogging: Reading, Commenting, Writing

Reading: Reading other people's blogs keeps you up-to-date on what others are interested in. Subscribe to blogs relevant to your industry. Search for relevant blogs at blogsearch.google.com. You can subscribe to and manage blogs at Google.com/reader.

Commenting: Commenting on other people's blogs builds relationships. You will get noticed by other bloggers and blog readers. Comments should increase the value of the article. Some things you can do in a comment are: share an example related to the article, add a point, add a useful link, disagree, or ask a question. When you post a comment, be sure to include your name and a link to your blog. You may just get the blogger to link back to your blog.

Writing. This is the part everyone worries about. What will I write about? How will I be able to keep up with it?

Here are some basic writing tips:

- Keep it short. It doesn't have to be a long post. One to three short paragraphs is more than enough.
- Make it specific. Don't be vague. People will get bored quickly and move on unless it's interesting and valuable to them.
- Make it interesting. Use images or formatting (bold, italics, lists) to create eye appeal.
- Don't be too self-promotional. Sure, it's your business. But this is not the place for a sales pitch. This is a place where people can come to be educated. They know where to find you once they want to do business.
- Create interesting titles. They can be funny, enticing (a list of 10 tips), or keyword rich for search engine optimization.
- Write regularly, at least weekly. I suggest at two to three times a week. Personally, I post each business day.

How Do I Promote My Blog?

- Email all your friends, family, colleagues and announce the launch of your blog. If you've already started blogging, send out an announcement at 6 months, 1 year, or at your 50th blog post.
- Trade guest articles with a similar blogger.
- Include a blog article in your newsletter and make sure to include a link back to your blog.
- Use your online business networking sites, such as Digg, Facebook, and LinkedIn, to let everyone know of your blog.
- At the end of your article, ask a question and ask for comments. Put it in bold.
- Create a board on Pinterest for all your blog posts. Be sure all your blog posts include an image.

What's next? So you got your free blog account set up. What's next? How often do you post and what do your write about? Don't lose any more valuable time. With your blog you can engage your prospects and clients in an informal conversation.

When to Post: If you are just starting out, you may post just once a month. But quickly increase it to weekly. Then I suggest you work up to at least three times weekly. Be consistent and post at the same days and times if at all possible.

Finding Time to Write

One of the most challenging obstacles you may face is finding the time to post blog entries on a regular basis. Remember that this is an important part of your business. It's an investment to help your business grow. Writing a blog entry or an article is an easy and simple way to spread your message and get prospects interested in your services. So don't put it off any longer.

You might get an idea while driving to an appointment but not have time to write an entry then. Make a note of your idea and come back to it when you do have time. Set specific times to write. Make a regular appointment with yourself for a specific block of time. Then stick to it.

What Do I Write About?

So now you're asking, 'what do I write about?' If you get stuck and can't think of anything, make it easy. Write a 'how-to' article or a 'ten tips' article. Here are some other suggestions:

Answer Questions with Blog Posts

You probably get questions from prospects and clients about your business. Use these questions and your answers as a basis for a blog post.

Invite Prospects to Write Guest Blog Posts

Ask prospects about their business. Everyone loves to talk about their business. Ask them to share their knowledge and lessons learned that would be relevant to your readers. Invite them to write a guest post.

Write About Your Client's Success

If you have a client that's doing very well, with permission, write a blog post about them. They'll probably send it to everyone they know. What better word of mouth could there be?

Ask Your Prospects for Feedback

Invite your readers to comment. Ask them for their opinions and feedback and post their comments. By including other people, you make your blog more engaging and interesting.

You get the added benefit of not having to work so hard to come up with content all the time.

Link to Your Prospect's Blog

If your prospect has a blog relevant to your industry, link to them.

Link to Resources and Other Relevant Articles

Some people are afraid that linking to other websites means your reader won't come back to yours. On the contrary, your readers will appreciate additional reading material on the subject and will visit your blog more frequently if they feel it is a good go-to resource.

In addition, linking to other bloggers increases the chances of them reading your blog and eventually linking back, which sends traffic directly to your blog and helps with search engine optimization.

It is not as difficult to come up with topics as you may think. Some other suggestions:

- Lists of 5 ideas, trends or thoughts
- A list of relevant links with a short comment on why you found each valuable
- Share a recent experience you had
- Comment on other blog articles you've read
- Turn a press release into a blog entry (again, tweak it so it's not too self-promotional)

Promoting Your Blog Promote Your Blog Via Email

If you send a monthly email newsletter, include a link to your blog. You may even include one of your blog posts in the newsletter. Have a prominent option to subscribe to your blog by email on your blog site and your website. Include your blog URL in your email signature.

Promote Your Blog Via Online Business Networking Sites

Use these sites to promote your blog. When you answer questions on LinkedIn, include a link to your blog. You can also put a small post in your 'status' message. If you frequent online business networking sites, people start to recognize you, trust you and inquire about your business. You need to be consistent and add value to the conversation. Show a genuine interest in helping other people.

Getting Your Blog Started Checklist
- Choose a platform, such as WordPress.
- Read and comment on relevant blogs (List 3-5 you will read and comment on weekly)
- Determine how often you want to post a blog entry (Daily, 3 times a week, weekly)
- Schedule time to blog (Every Friday from 3-4 write 3 blog posts for coming week)
- Start a list of topics to write about (Answer client questions, invite guest bloggers to post, write about your client's success, etc.)
- Promote your blog (List ways you will do this: via email, on networking sites, Facebook, Twitter, etc.)

Social Media

Social networking is an important strategy to market your business. Used appropriately, social networking can be effective in getting your message out to your prospects. By creating an online presence at targeted social networks, your prospects can begin to get to know you, learn to trust you and eventually turn to you for your products and services.

Social media may include any online forums or social networks where you and your prospects and clients can interact. There are literally hundreds. I recommend you choose a few that you actively participate in so that you don't become overwhelmed. The ones most important to a Chief Virtual Officer are, in my opinion, Facebook, Twitter, LinkedIn, Google+, and Pinterest.

How do you find time for social media? It's easy to spend hours on Twitter and Facebook and then not get any work done. I suggest you schedule 30 minutes each day in valuable participation on social media sites. Set a timer and spend 10 minutes at Twitter, 10 minutes on Facebook, 5 minutes on LinkedIn and 5 minutes on Pinterest. When your timer goes off at 30 minutes, stop and get back to work.

Use the space below to make notes of how you will implement social media marketing strategies in your business.

Newsletter

Staying in touch with prospects and clients keeps you at the top of their mind when they are thinking about who to contact for assistance. A newsletter is an excellent way to stay in touch with prospects and clients. Provide valuable information and resources that your clients and prospects can use in their business and they will look forward to your newsletter.

There are many different email management systems you can use to manage your newsletter. Do some research to see which one best fits your needs and budget while still giving you room to grow.

Email Management Systems
- Constant Contact - http://www.constantcontact.com/
- iContact - http://www.icontact.com/
- MyEmma - http://myemma.com/
- Infusion Soft - http://www.infusionsoft.com/

Article Writing

Writing articles is an excellent way for prospects to come to know you and your services. Articles build your reputation and credibility as an expert in your niche. You can reprint your articles on your website and in your newsletter as well. It's not as difficult as you might think to write an article. Often you can take a blog entry and expand it into an article.

There are literally hundreds of places you can submit your articles at no charge. The **Appendix** includes an extensive list where you can submit articles.

It is vital that you proofread your articles before posting. If possible, ask someone else to proofread them as well. Double check your spelling and grammar. Don't rely solely on your software's spell check capabilities.

Marketing Your Services Checklist

- Website
- Photo
- Rates
- Content and keywords specific to target market and niche
- Free Report
- Blog
- Social Media: Facebook, Twitter, LinkedIn. Google Plus
- Newsletter
- Article Writing and Submission
- Press Releases
- Networking at local meetup groups
- Printed Marketing Materials
- Flyers
- Brochures
- Postcards

Review: Marketing Your Services

Have you set up systems do market your services using these strategies?

- Website
- Free Report
- Blog
- Social Media
- Newsletter
- Article Writing

Referrals and Testimonials

Referrals are an excellent way to get new clients. So how do you get people to refer you? Provide excellent service! You will find that when your clients are excited about working with you, they will refer you to their friends and business associates without your having to ask them. Also, if you start referring work to people you know, you will find that they reciprocate.

Personally, I don't believe in paid referrals. However, I do like to reward those who have referred a prospect. If the prospect becomes a paying client and the referrer is my client, I give them additional hours of my services at no charge. If the referrer is not my client, I send some sort of thank you. Even if the prospect does not become a client, be sure to thank the referrer in some way.

Testimonials help prospects see how you work with your clients. Once you have a few testimonials, ask these clients if they are willing to speak with prospects about how you work with them. Then if a prospect asks, you'll have the names and contact information of a few clients for your prospects to talk with.

Getting a testimonial is not difficult. Usually in an email at some point your client will make positive comments about the services you are providing. Take these comments and compile them into a testimonial. Then send that to your client and ask if you can use their comments as a testimonial on your website and in other marketing materials.

Let them know you will include a link to their website. Since you've done all the hard work in compiling the testimonial, I've found that clients are more than willing to allow you to use their compiled comments as a testimonial. They may wish to reword it some and that's fine.

Sub-Contracting

There may come a time when you have more work than you alone can handle. You may consider sub-contracting some of the work to another virtual assistant. Perhaps your client asks you to do a new task for which you don't have the skills. This portion of the work you could also sub-contract out.

You may also want to start out as a subcontractor to another virtual assistant. This may be a great way to get started in the business. Keep in mind, though, that the rate you will be paid as a subcontractor may be considerably less than the primary VA. Be sure to get a signed contract detailing the work you will do, the rate you will get paid and how you will get paid.

Savvy Subcontracting - Gain and Retain Clients by Subcontracting

Colleen specializes in subcontracting and assisting other VAs looking for subcontracted work.

Colleen's website: http://www.savvysubcontracting.com/

Collaborating with Other Chief Virtual Officers

There are two very good reasons to collaborate with other Chief Virtual Officers.

1. Pool resources
2. Combat loneliness

Pool resources: As mentioned in the section on subcontracting, there may be a time when you are asked to do a task for which you don't have the skills. If you've established relationships with other Chief Virtual Officers, you may be able to collaborate with them to get the task done for your client. Instead of telling your client that you are unable to do the task, or worse yet, saying you will and then being unable to, you can call upon one of the other Chief Virtual Officers you already have an established relationship with. I've even worked with clients that have several VAs working for them at once; each one specializes in a particular task.

Combat loneliness: Yes, you do work well independently. However, there are times when it can get a bit lonely and you wish you had someone to brainstorm with. Building relationships with other Chief Virtual Officers can combat the loneliness and gives you a way to brainstorm ideas. Though there are lots of places to do this online, meeting in person and having a face-to-face conversation can be very rewarding.

If your area does not have a local VA meetup group, perhaps you can start one.

There are also Virtual Assistants Meetup Groups online where you can meet other local Virtual Assistants, discuss business practices and unwind from the everyday demands of a Virtual Assistant. Search for one in your area here: http://virtualasst.meetup.com/

The Next Step

Congratulations! You have finished Succeed as a *Chief Virtual Officer: Setting Up a Successful Virtual Assistant Business* and are ready to start your career as a Chief Virtual Officer . . . or are you?

I certainly hope this book has provided you with valuable information and tools to assist you in your decision to become a Chief Virtual Officer. However you may still feel the need for additional support. In addition to the resources you will find in the next section, we have the additional support you need.

You will want to be sure to add to your library of business books our book, *The Commonsense Virtual Assistant - Becoming an Entrepreneur, Not an Employee.* Order your copy for $19.95 at http://chiefvirtualofficer.com.

Become a fan of The Commonsense Virtual Assistant on Facebook at http://www.facebook.com/CommonsenseVirtualAssistant.

Follow Sue on Twitter at http://twitter.com/sueawesome. She posts tips for Chief Virtual Officers and you can find these using the hash tag #CVOtips.

Read the Chief Virtual Officer blog where you will find valuable information on how to succeed in business at http://chiefvirtualofficer.com/blog/.

Follow Sue on Pinterest: http://www.pinterest.com/sueawesome/articles-for-virtual-assistants/

Follow Sue on Google+: https://plus.google.com/+SueCanfield/

Useful Online Tools

The number of online tools you can choose to use in your business are innumerable and continually growing. Research the tools that will work best for your business. If there's a free trial version, take advantage of it to find out if it is the right tool for you.

Online Tools Sue Recommends

Echo Sign - EchoSign.com - get your contracts signed electronically; no need to print, sign and mail back a copy.

Central Desktop - CentralDesktop.com - a great tool allowing you to store and share information with your clients.

Box.net - Box.net - store files to share with clients.

Google - Google.com - Google is continually adding new services. Use Google Alerts to track what's going on in the industry, set up a profile page, use Google's email, create and share documents, use their reader to track the blogs you read and comment on, use Google Talk to communicate with clients free.

Skype -Skype.com - an affordable telephone solution to communicate with clients.

Copilot - Copilot.com - an affordable remote control solution when you need to help your client with something on their computer.

Chrometa - Chrometa.com - time tracking software.

Appendix

Note: The samples in the appendix are designed as a starting point only. We chose not to provide templates you could copy and paste and just put in your own information. We want you to really think about what you are creating.

You need to think about your particular business, the specific services you offer, and your specific marketing strategies as you use these samples. This will help you come to an even better understanding of your business and how best you can serve your clients.

Sample Marketing Plan

Sample Marketing Calendar

Sample of Pre-Contract Questionnaire

Sample Services Contract

Sample Blogging Questionnaire

Sample Self Promotion Questionnaire

Sue L Canfield

Sample Marketing Plan
for

Company Name

Part 1 - Goal: explain your specific goals for the year, including dollar amounts, number of clients, etc.

By focusing on one marketing strategy each month, we will double our gross income to $50,000; have 25 names on our client list by December 31, 2014, and have work for at least 2 team members working a total of 20 hours per week.

We want to increase our exposure and income. We will be able to provide part-time work for other virtual assistants.

Part 2 - Target Market: explain who your target market is and what you do for them.

Our target market is solo service providers. We help them maintain their energy and excitement for what they do by taking on the tasks that drain them of energy. Our specific niche is online marketing for service providers.

Part 3 - Marketing Strategies: a paragraph noting the specific marketing strategies you will use throughout the year.

The marketing weapons we will use in 2014 are:
1. Website 2. Blog 3. Articles 4. Social Networks 5.

Brochures 6. Postcards 7. Ebook 8. Networking 9. Thank you cards

Part 4 - Budget: a final paragraph about your marketing budget and any marketing tools you have created.

We have budgeted $1200 total for the year, $100 per month. We are able to budget such a small amount because we can do most of the work ourselves. The only cost would be printing postcards and brochures, postage and supplies.

We have created a marketing calendar separately that describes what we will do each month and how.

Sue L Carfield

Sample Marketing Calendar
Month

Marketing Weapon Details +/-

What worked & how to improve for next time

- **January** Brochures - Create, print, distribute 20 brochures
- **February** Article - Submit an article to minimum of 3 sites
- **March** Postcards -Create, print, distribute 20 postcards
- **April** Blog - Blog each work day on both blogs
- **May** Social Networking - Update profiles on all social media sites
- **June** Website - Update website
- **July** Ebook - Create PDF about online marketing
- **August** Postcards -Create, print, distribute 20 postcards
- **September** Article - Submit an article to minimum of 3 sites
- **October** Network - Have coffee with at least 2 people I met at networking events this year
- **November** Blog - Blog each work day
- **December** Cards - Send out thank you cards to every client/prospect

Sample of Pre-Contract Questionnaire

VA Company Name

- Address
- Phone
- Email
- Website

Pre-Consultation Questionnaire

Are you ready to take the next step and find out how I can assist you? If so, please complete the following questionnaire and return it to me. I will then contact you to setup an appointment for a consultation. I look forward to helping you grow your business.

Prospect Name:

Company Name:

Address: City: State: Zip: Physical Address: City: State: Zip:

Phone: Fax: Cell: Email: Web site: Industry: Years in Business:

Briefly describe your business: Please provide a description of the project or services you are interested in: Please list any questions you may have regarding my services: Please provide us with three dates and times in which you would be available for a phone consultation: 1. 2. 3.

How did you hear about us? : (if referred by someone, please provide their name)

Sue L Canfield

Sample Services Contract

Sue L Canfield Chief Virtual Officer
sChiefVirtualOfficer.com

124 W Eau Claire Street, Rice Lake, WI 54868
(715) 296-0347

Sue@chiefvirtualofficer.com

Client: ABC Company Dated: February 2, 2014

1. Authorization

The above named client is engaging Sue L Canfield as an independent contractor for the specific purpose of performing administrative tasks as outlined in 'Scope'. Hereafter, the client will be known as the "Client" and Sue L Canfield will be known as the "Contractor."

2. Scope (Detailed description of work to be done)

3. Financial Obligations The Contractor will be paid at the rate of_____ per _____ for work performed in accordance with this agreement. The Contractor will submit an itemized statement setting forth the time spent and services rendered.

- Per project fees require a 50% deposit before work begins. The balance will be billed upon completion of the project and is due upon receipt.
- Retainer fees are prepaid monthly and due the 1st of each month. Retainer fees are non-refundable. Unused hours will not roll over.

Payment can be made by check payable to Sue L Canfield or by PayPal to PayPal@[company name].

Payments are due upon receipt of invoice unless otherwise indicated.

4. Work Flow

Contractor will keep a log detailing the type of work done and the hours worked. This log will be used as a basis for billing hourly Clients. For Clients with a Retainer Agreement, the log will ensure that the time allotted is not exceeded.

5. Policies and Procedures

The best way for Client to contact Contractor is by email at contact@ChiefVirtualOfficer.com. This address will also copy Contractor's team members; so if for some reason Contractor is unavailable, one of Contractor's team members may reply. Contractor normally reads and responds to emails during normal working hours at 10 am, 1 pm, and 3:30 pm PST. Contractor's policy is to reply to any contact within 24 hours during normal working hours, excluding weekends. Client is expected to give Contractor a minimum of 48 hours' notice of any rush job to be done and an additional rush fee may apply. Contractor's normal working hours are Monday through Thursday, 10-12 am and 1-4 pm Pacific Standard Time (PST). Contractor will notify Client in advance of time taken off for vacations. Any prepaid blocks of time must be used within 90 days of date of contract unless otherwise specified. Unused amounts of time will not rollover. Client understands that Contractor may use sub-contractors to complete projects and

Contractor is responsible for paying sub-contractors. Client payments should be made by check payable to Sue L Canfield or by PayPal to PayPal@[company name]. Our customer service policy can be read here: http://chiefvirtualofficer.com/chief_virtual_officer_philosophy.php.

6. Confidentiality

During the term of this Agreement, Contractor shall act exclusively in the best interest of Client. Contractor acknowledges that it may have access to information which is non-public, confidential and proprietary in nature. Such confidential information may include, but is not limited to, trade secrets, business plans, copyrights, logos, trademarks, financial and operational information and membership lists. Contractor expressly agrees not to use or disclose such information in any manner or for any purpose at any time during or after the effective term of this Agreement, except as required by law or as required during the course of Contractor's work for Client, unless authorized in writing by Client. Upon expiration or termination of this Agreement, Contractor shall return any such information to Client. Likewise, the Client agrees that it will not convey any Confidential information obtained about the Contractor to another party.

7. Termination

This Agreement may be terminated by Client, with or without cause, upon written notice to

Contractor. In the event that this agreement is canceled at the request of the Client, the Contractor shall have the right to retain any prepaid monies. This Agreement may be terminated by Contractor with a 30-day written notice. In the event this agreement is canceled by Contractor, Contractor will fulfill any outstanding obligations within 30- days of written notice of cancellation.

8. Independent Contractor

Contractor is an independent contractor, to whom Client shall have no obligation as an employer. Client will not pay or withhold, and Contractor will hold Client harmless from costs for employee benefits, employee taxes, insurance, and other costs typically arising from an employee-employer relationship. Contractor shall pay its own expenses, including but not limited to all salaries and commissions to Contractor's employees, occupational taxes in the form of licenses to engage in or to conduct business, and all taxes including, but not limited to taxes that may be assessed on the personal property and equipment of Contractor's used in the conduct of Contractor's business. Any costs or expenses incurred by Contractor in the performance of its duties, and all such costs and expenses shall be borne by Contractor. Neither party is authorized by the other under this Agreement to act on behalf of or in the name of the other party or any of their affiliates or subsidiaries. Neither party shall have the authority to bind the other in contract, debt or otherwise.

9. Arbitration

Any disputes in excess of $1,000 (or the maximum limit for small claims court) arising out of this Agreement shall be submitted to binding arbitration before a mutually agreed upon Arbitrator suitor pursuant to the rules of the American Arbitration Association. The Arbitrator's award shall be final, and judgment may be entered in any court having jurisdiction thereof. The Client shall pay all arbitration and court costs, reasonable attorney's fees and legal interest on any award or judgment in favor of the Contractor.

10. Entire Understanding

This contract and any Appendices attached thereto constitute the sole agreement between the Contractor and the Client regarding this project. It becomes effective only when signed by both parties. It is the spirit of this agreement that this will be a mutually beneficial arrangement for the Client and the Contractor.

Both parties warrant that they have read and understand the terms set forth in this agreement. This agreement shall be governed and construed in accordance with the laws of the State of California.

On behalf of the Client _____

Client Signature   Date _____

On behalf of the Contractor _____

Sue L Canfield   Date _____

Thank you for choosing Sue L Canfield, Chief Virtual Officer!

Sue L Garfield

Sample Blogging Questionnaire
Name:

Business Name:

Industry:

Address:

Phone:

Email:

Website:

Briefly describe your business:

How long have you been in business?

How would you describe your target market or ideal client? Be as specific as possible.

What are the challenges, issues, problems your clients have?

What results do your clients want?

What solution will you deliver?

Tell me a little bit about yourself. What types of things do you enjoy doing, hobbies, etc.? (You will learn that finding out about your client's personal interests can help you market better to them.)

Where do you see your business in one year; five years?

What specific goals to you want to accomplish by blogging?

How much time each month do you want to spend on blogging?

How much have you budgeted monthly for blogging?

Do you have a website address? Website address:

If yes, how often do you update it?

Do you have a blog? Blog address:

If yes, how often do you post entries?

Where is it hosted?

Do you have an e-newsletter?

If yes, how often do you send it out?

Any other comments or questions you have about blogging:

Sample Self Promotion Questionnaire

Name:

Business Name:

Industry:

Address:

Phone:

Email:

Website:

Briefly describe your business:

How long have you been in business?

How would you describe your target market or ideal client? Be as specific as possible.

What are the challenges, issues, problems your clients have?

What results do your clients want?

What solution will you deliver?

Tell me a little bit about yourself. What types of things do you enjoy doing, hobbies, etc.? (You will learn that finding out about your client's personal interests can help you market better to them.)

Where do you see your business in one year; five years?

What specific goals do you want to accomplish by using this self- promotion plan?

How much time each month do you want to spend on self-promotion?

How much have you budgeted monthly for self-promotion?

Do you have a website address?

Website address:

If yes, how often do you update it?

Do you have a blog?

Blog address:

Do you have an e-newsletter?

If yes, how often do you send it out?

Circle the top 5 marketing tools you'd like to implement:

- Marketing plan
- Marketing calendar
- Defining your niche market
- Your brand identity
- Logo
- Stationery
- Business cards
- Word-of-mouth
- Club/Association memberships
- Free consultations
- Free seminars and workshops
- Free demonstrations
- Free samples

- Success stories
- Service
- Follow-up
- Column in a publication
- Article in a publication
- Speaker at any club
- Newsletter
- Benefits list
- Media contacts
- Referral program
- Guarantee
- Gift certificates
- Brochures
- Electronic brochures
- Networking
- Online marketing
- Prospect mailing lists
- Testimonials

Final Note:

I want this to be the single most essential virtual assistant book on the market. Tell us what else it needs to make that happen.

I would love to hear from you! Feel free to contact me with questions, comments and suggestions. Your feedback is greatly appreciated. Thank you!

Contact Sue

Sue@ChiefVirtualOfficer.com (715) 296-0347

http://ChiefVirtualOfficer.com

BONUS #1

The following is a bonus document you are free to use. Its purpose is to help business owners understand the value of using a virtual assistant.

11 Ways a Virtual Assistant Will Help You Get More Done

Wouldn't it be great if you could get talented professional help, but only as much as you needed?

Save Money & Increase Efficiency Using Pay-As-You-Go Shared Employees

Small businesses don't have money to spend the way big business seems to. As you struggle to make ends meet, you're stuck with tasks you really don't enjoy and, as a result, probably aren't doing as well as they should be done. You know you can't afford a full-time assistant, but you also know you can't keep juggling all that other work with the stuff that makes you money—the stuff that made you start your own business in the first place.

Wouldn't it be great if you could get talented professional help, but only as much as you needed? Sort of like renting an employee, the way you rent a projector for your big presentation?

You can. These shared, pay-as-you go professionals are called virtual assistants, or virtual office professionals. And here's the kicker: they're not employees, they're entrepreneurs themselves, so not only do they really understand your challenges, but they don't come with all the extra costs in money and time that come with hiring an employee.

This report, "11 Ways a Virtual Assistant Will Help You Get More Done", tells you exactly what to look for in a virtual office professional, describes the kinds of tasks you can and can't expect them to manage for you, and gives you tips on how to make the best use of your virtual assistant. To begin, we'll even explain what on earth 'virtual' means, and why it matters. What's All This 'Virtual' Stuff, Anyway?

Maybe you've heard about virtual reality. You've certainly heard about virtual assistants, even if it was just in the introduction to this report.

Get the best help at a fair price

In this context 'virtual' means 'not in the same physical location' or 'remotely, using the internet' or something that makes it clear that a virtual assistant can be located anywhere in the world, and still work closely with you to get tasks done.

We've been asked, more than once, to help folks find a virtual assistant in 'their area'. It's been a challenge explaining that it just doesn't matter where a virtual assistant lives in relation to their client. The internet lives everywhere, right?

Even when physical documents must change hands, it's fairly simple (and, in fact, cost-effective) to use FedEx or some other overnight or confirmed- delivery service. However, it's often very efficient to make digital versions of those documents (by scanning, for instance) and use email or online file sharing to hand them off.

Having access to a virtual workforce allows you a nearly infinite pool of professionals to choose from. Imagine; you're not limited to administrative professionals in your locality (which if you're in a small town or rural area can be a real problem.) Instead, if you find a VA on the other side of the world, as long as you can work around the time zone difference (and, trust us, you can) you can get the best help at a fair price.

What to Look for in a Virtual Office Professional

It's pretty easy to assess the empirical qualities of an administrative assistant: typing speed and accuracy, experience with heavy phone use, bookkeeping or accounting knowledge, things like that. Keep in mind, though, that you're not hiring a secretary. You're forming a professional alliance with another entrepreneur.

A virtual assistant should be able to demonstrate proficiency in administrative tasks, but they should also be able to tell you about their business and marketing plans, their growth strategy, their sales process, and all the other business functions you know are required to be an entrepreneur.

If your conversations with a prospective virtual assistant make you think 'hireling' rather than 'peer' you should revisit either your attitude or their presentation. If they think of themselves as an employee, you need to consider whether or not they'll be the self-starting knowledgeable partner you really need.

Of course, consider that you may be stuck in the old-school thinking that administrative tasks are handled by a secretary, sent at random from the secretarial pool on the sixth floor. Stop. If you want an employee to manage, find one and accept the extra management effort required. If you're looking for a highly skilled professional to help you get more done and grow your business, make sure that you're seeing these prospects as partners in a joint venture, not an underling who dances to your tune.

Look for entrepreneurial excellence along with the administrative skills which should be a given.

What Can't a VA Do?

That's really not the right title, because if you happen to have a VA who's local, they can pop into your office to take care of tasks that require physical presence. But the reality is, most virtual assistants really like the 'virtual' part of their business. Asking them to come in to do filing or manual bookkeeping or some other on-site task is usually not the best use of their time and skills, and not a good match for your needs.

So, what can you expect to hand off to a virtual assistant? To some extent, this may depend on their area of focus and expertise. While nearly all virtual assistants have a broad range of administrative skills, most have a niche they focus on. If your VA has a strong accounting background, they're a great candidate to manage your bookkeeping. If they're a web developer in another life, they should be able to take over your website updates and modifications without much effort. If they have experience in sales or customer service, they just might have great phone skills, allowing you to use them for appointment setting, event reminder calls to clients, or other phone work.

What may take you hours to complete because of all the distractions and necessary projects that have to be done, a virtual assistant can get done in an hour or so.

How to Make the Best Use of Your Virtual Assistant

Hopefully we've established that your virtual assistant or virtual office professional is a peer, another entrepreneur with whom you'll develop a close trusting relationship. Also, that their physical location is, really, immaterial to the business process.

Here's the single greatest tool you can employ to make excellent use of this professional's talents, skills, and knowledge:

Trust.

Consider: when you have trust in a business relationship, things move faster. They cost less. There's less frustration. Trust creates speed and efficiency. Trust fosters contentment.

If you expect your VA to fill in a time sheet, detailing the time they've spent on every project, you're treating them like an employee, and not a very trusted one (we personally believe time clocks should be abolished, even for hourly employees, but then, we also believe we should all be working toward not paying or being paid by the hour; heretical, we know.)

Treat your virtual office professional the way you would any trusted vendor. Don't announce deadlines, discuss time-based goals which work for everyone. Remember that you're not their only client—but then, you have more than one client and you take good care of all of them, right?

Communicate clearly and frequently. Working virtually means you must be much clearer in your instructions, and you must follow up (checking, not pushing) a little more frequently. Never assume. Even with that 'trust' thing, trust, but verify, until the relationship has blossomed to the point that you no longer feel the need to verify. Ask for reports at reasonable intervals, and give feedback on what you consider 'reasonable' so your partner can update you more frequently, or less frequently.

Assume that you're dealing with a professional who knows how to get the job done and who will do the right thing for a fair price.

Remember to visit ChiefVirtualOfficer.com for even more information about finding and working with the right virtual office professional

Learning to let go, to trust someone else with your precious business tasks and data, is the biggest challenge to working with a virtual assistant. Do your homework before you establish the relationship, and you'll get to a solid trusting partnership much more quickly.

The List: 11 Ways a Virtual Assistant Can Help You Get More Done

Each of the 11 points below is really just an overview to spark some thinking. If you've partnered with the right VA, do yourselves a favor and simply offer them any task or project you'd like to hand off. They'll let you know if it's a fit for them, and if it's not, they'll probably offer to bring in another VA who specializes in exactly what needs to be done.

But, just to jump-start your thinking- outside-the-box process, here's the list:

1. Compared to a traditional employee your setup and training costs are reduced. A virtual assistant doesn't take up office space. They don't need you to buy a computer, put in a desk, set up a phone and filing cabinet and all that. They're essentially a drop-in module, ready to work after a brief

orientation to your business needs. The saved time, effort and money can be applied directly to other projects and tasks you should handle yourself.

2. Here's the obvious benefit: once you hand off those tasks to the VA, you're free to do the things that add directly to your bottom line.

3. A virtual assistant is a business owner and can provide business feedback. They can act as a sounding board for any business ideas you've got, often offering a new and different perspective. They'll get to know your business, but retain the fresh perspective of an outsider—the best of both worlds.

4. A virtual assistant is self-starting. There's no need to micro- manage (always a bad idea) because they're a professional, an entrepreneur, not a trainee.

5. A virtual assistant allows you to work in the manner that's most efficient for you. No longer do you have to type a letter when you'd rather dictate it. No longer do you have to type, when you can write by hand faster. Work in the way that's most natural to you, and allow a professional to translate it to whatever medium is appropriate.

6. And just the opposite of #5, sometimes working with another professional will help nudge you out of your comfort zone, help you see things differently. It can make the perceived risks of 'new & different' less scary

7. Fewer lost opportunities. Sharing your workload and marketing efforts allows you to keep better tabs on your follow-up process, to be aware of and available for new opportunities. A good VA and institute automation and efficiency tools and processes which help get your sales funnel filled and flowing, and allows you to focus on the bits which are uniquely and best done by you.

8. A virtual assistant who's good at marketing, social media, etc. can help spark innovation, creating new ways to find clients, sell more to existing clients, or create other excellent ideas to help you grow.

9. A virtual assistant with organizational skills can pay for themselves just in time saved looking for information. Did you know that the average person spends three hours per week looking for paper documents? What about other information that you put 'somewhere safe' and can't find? If you save 5 hours per week of your own time because you've offloaded this information storage and retrieval process to an expert, how quickly could you pay for their services in saved time and new income generated in that saved time?

10. Self-Justification: when you have access to a trusted professional, you're likely to hand off those little 'someday' tasks you'd otherwise put off 'til they were like those moldy leftovers in the back of the fridge. We all have those little nagging tasks that we just don't feel like doing. They never

float to the top of the list. Eventually, instead of being a simple task, one of two things happens: they become an emergency, with the accompanying stress and additional expenses in time, effort, and sometimes money; or, they drop off the list, never to be done. (Organizational tip: if you're really never going to do something because it's really not important, take it off the list now, not next month or, worse, next year.)

That's ten very good reasons to investigate how a virtual office professional could be the best thing that ever happened to your business. but just in case you still need a little convincing, here's #11, a mini-report all its own:

Instead of focusing on gaining new clients to increase your business, focus on contributing value to others.

Increase Your Energy and Your Profits While Contributing More

Do you want to grow your business and increase your profits and at the same time increase your energy? Of course you do! Yet you may find yourself spending more and more time and energy on tasks you don't enjoy and that don't directly increase your profits. How can you still accomplish those things while increasing your energy and profits? Get professional help!

Two questions to ask yourself to determine what tasks you need to get help with are:

1. What are the things you do that drain you of energy? We all do things we really enjoy and that energize us. We also do things that tend to drain our energy.

2. What are the things you do that don't directly increase your profits? You know—those tasks that have to be done in a business but don't directly bring in income.

Once you've identified the things that drain you of energy and that don't directly increase your profits, you're ready to call in professional help. A virtual assistant can take on those tasks, leaving you with the tasks that you feel energized about and that contribute directly to your bottom line.

But what's this about contributing more? Most service providers, such as consultants, coaches, therapists and others, realize their business is all about making a contribution. They are focused on helping individuals develop, grow, change, and improve.

Any business owner can increase their profits by gaining new clients. The key here is to approach this with a new mindset. Instead of focusing on gaining new clients to increase your business, focus on contributing value to others. The increased business and new clients will come.

Think about how you market to your clients. Is your focus on what you do and what your services you provide? The key is to focus on our prospects and clients, on their needs, who they are, what challenges they face, and what benefits they will receive by using your services.

Marketing now needs to focus more on building relationships. That's why we've seen an increase in businesses using social sites such as LinkedIn, Facebook, Twitter, and Pinterest. This is a way to begin building relationships and providing valuable education to prospects. Use these sites to provide resources and referrals. Be involved and participate in a meaningful way. Building relationships at these sites can build trust and at some point you'll find people asking more about what you can do for them.

Another way to contribute is to write articles and reports, such as this one, and distribute them freely. They not only increase your credibility, they give your prospects valuable information and a way for them to learn more about you and your services. But Wait; There's More!

It should be clear by now that there are far more than eleven ways a virtual office professional can help you get more done, save you time, money, effort, and frustration, and help grow your business.

Bonus #2

The following is an excerpt of The Commonsense Virtual Assistant – Becoming An Entrepreneur, Not an Employye.

Chapter Seven: Customer Service

Nearly everything I have to say about customer service is covered in the sections on how people think. This section will focus on actual customer interaction; the stuff most of us think of when we think of customer service.

What Do You Expect?

I've rattled on endlessly about treating your customers like grown-ups, like special honored guests. Here's the other side of that coin: they're not the professionals; you are.

Don't expect your clientele to understand the technical jargon common to your industry. If I mention 'hosting', 'IP address', or 'domain name' to most of my clients, I get blank stares. That's okay; if they didn't need technical assistance I'd be out of work.

Stop and think about the terminology that's specific to your industry. If you're not absolutely positive your gramma (or better still, your neighbor's gramma) would understand it, find a simpler way to say it. It's fine to educate your customers, but don't expect them to educate themselves just to do business with you.

Remember, making people feel dumb is not going to earn their business. Make them comfortable. That means not making them ask **you what you're talking about.**

Close to You

It's common for the owner of the company to become less accessible as it grows. For you, that's a good thing, because you get to focus on what you're best at, letting others handle what they're best at.

But don't make the mistake of making your customers talk to the busboy if you're the one grilling their steak (or veggie kabob, if that's your preference.)

It's common corporate thinking to have 'customer service' folks answering all the phones. You may have an administrative type or assistant managing customer interaction. If they've read this book and really care about people, you're probably in good shape. But don't isolate the customers from the people who are actually working on their solutions.

This is another way to differentiate yourself. Most companies make sure their technicians aren't bothered by customers. It's partly to keep the talent working, and partly because the talent often has minimal social skills. Make sure your talent (including you) knows that these customers allow us the privilege of being in business. Teach them whatever they need to excel at customer interaction. Now your clientele feels privileged because they get a glimpse into the inner workings of your company—and, just a little bit, it becomes their company.

This also makes responding to customers faster. Instead of waiting on hold for a customer service queue, you have a whole company full of folks who can help with most things. Even if it takes a call back from the right person, getting some kind of response from a real human, right away, makes all the difference in the world.

Earning Tips

No, not tips on earning. Learning to think in the moment, getting instant feedback on how you're doing.

Imagine if the only way your company made money was tips, based entirely on the quality of your customer service, not your product. The servers in your favorite restaurant don't have to imagine. The bulk of their income has nothing to do with the food they carried to the table.

This is a huge customer service advantage. Imagine if, after every single transaction, the customer told you in simple black and white terms how they felt about your service? Bellhops, skycaps and waiters know. They get a tip or they don't. If they do, it's big or it's not. If they're smart, they'll do more of what earns big tips, and less of what got none.

Every single customer interaction, you should know whether you've earned a tip, and how big it would be.

Ask. Yes, talk to your customers some more. And don't wait to mail some questionnaire through the mail or for them to take your online survey. If you can, ask before they pay your bill or hand their credit card to the cashier. If you can't do that, call (don't email) and ask them how you did. Ask them, point blank, if they'd recommend you to others. If not, find out what was broken and fix it. (Read up on the concept of Net Promoter Score and see how it can help you think like a waiter.)

Sue L Canfield

Contact

For more for help finding or qualifying a virtual assistant, contact:

Web: www.ChiefVirtualOfficer.com   Email: Sue@ChiefVirtualOfficer.com   Phone: (715)296-0347

About the Author

For nearly 35 years Sue Canfield, Chief Virtual Officer, has helped small business owners with administrative tasks. She also co-authored the book, *The Commonsense Virtual Assistant - Becoming an Entrepreneur, Not an Employee*, to help virtual assistants understand what it takes to be a business owner.

Sue L Carfield

www.ingramcontent.com/pod-product-compliance
Lightning Source LLC
Chambersburg PA
CBHW051725170526
45167CB00002B/803